Against the Wind

A Motorcycle Ride

Dale Arenson

Also by the author;

Hangmen, Riding with an Outlaw Motorcycle Club in the Old Days.
Available on Amazon.

Table of Contents

Introduction

This is a story of a trip on a motorcycle. Not just any motorcycle, but on a chopper similar to what I rode in the past. It is not an old one however, it was built in 2007, but it looks and sounds like the bikes I rode in the old days. Rough riding and a lot of vibration. Back then my 'old' 1951 Panhead was only eighteen years old and so was I.

And now, not just any rider. An old rider who has spent most of his life on motorcycles. They have always been there. All kinds of bikes, but this trip is different, the bike is different, and the time... while today, seems different.

In some ways this was a journey into the past, reliving the memories of traveling alone on a motorcycle, while enjoying the present moment.

H.G Wells sat in his time machine and moved through time, but not space; I was riding on mine through space and time. Only much slower.

Back then, I had no money and did not know where I was going. Now I am retired and have a little money, and still, I only know where I've been. Knowing where I'm going, still seems to be a bit of a challenge. But on this ride, I had maps. And was not in a hurry, it was about the ride more than the destination.

I wanted to enjoy going down the highway with only short-term goals, like finding gas, dinner and maybe a couple of beers, before finding a place to sleep.

Get up the next day and repeat the process. Relax and ride, stop and smell the coffee and the gasoline. And if you're lucky, maybe a few roses along the way.

Journeys are mostly enhanced by the people you meet along the way. That is where most of the interesting stories come from. Unfortunately, I am not an outgoing person and meeting people does not come easy to me, but who knows, I could get lucky.

The interstate would have been too easy and you would not see as much. Just used to get somewhere, nobody rides the interstate for fun, and the gas stops are like airline terminals. Full of people and merchandise to sell.
The two-lane back roads are a slower pace, and a slower way of life.

Day 1

Arizona

Leaving

It doesn't get any better than this.

It's an overused phrase, we hear it all the time. But on the first day, leaving Arizona and heading to Oklahoma, I was thinking that a lot.

Riding along the Mogollon Rim, looking out at the vast expanses of forest and trees, it was hard to keep in mind that I was still in Arizona. It looked more like parts of Wyoming or Montana.

We were on a new adventure, the bike and I. It was running great, purring along like it was happy to be out of the garage and didn't want to go back.

Being the middle of June, the temperature was perfect, about 75 degrees because of the altitude. Not sweating or freezing. Any day on a motorcycle is a good day, but when the weather is on your side, it's a great day.

For most of the day I had a tailwind which feels almost like riding in a bubble. On a bike like this Ultima chopper with no wind protection, that's a big plus. I literally felt that I was gone with the wind. The wind was with me and helping me along.

This was my first long trip on this bike, and I was surprisingly comfortable, leaning back on the gear I had strapped on the short sissy bar. With my legs stretched out, feet on the forward pegs, it felt more like a Lazy Boy chair that had a massaging vibration mode. You controlled the intensity of the massage with your right hand on the throttle.

Coming into Payson, traffic was light and kept moving smoothly. I considered stopping for lunch at one of the many cafes, diners, or fast-food places, or maybe a hot dog at one of the gas station / convenience stores. Instead, I took a detour on Tyler Parkway and avoided most of the town.

Back on Hwy 260 I rode though Star Valley, after which the road opened into the national forest and turned into a divided four lane highway, running fast and smooth through sweeping turns.

Life was good!

Peering between the ape-hanger handlebars, I enjoyed the view as the road curved one way and then the other. Mountains and pine trees provided splendid views all around. The mountain air smelled fresh and clean.

East of Payson Highway 260 enters the Apache-Sitgreaves National Forest. I leaned left and right, following the turns as the road carved through the scenic forested terrain.

Fifty-one years ago, I spent most of the year of 1970 riding alone on my Harley Davidson, Pan-Head chopper, mostly in Washington state and Oregon. Being from Southern California, I was a long way from home.

It was a special time, although it was just past "The Sixties," it was still that same atmosphere. And traveling on a motorcycle was something Hollywood made movies and television shows about. Easy Rider and Then Came Bronson had just come out the year before.

I don't remember those shows having any effect on me, I thought Bronson was a square on a stock bike, and although I liked the bikes in Easy Rider, the characters weren't like the tough guys I knew and rode with.

These days however, I have a lot of respect for the movie and TV shows, because they portrayed a lifestyle of traveling on a bike and brought it to the attention of the non-riding public. They helped to change the motorcycle world.

I've often wondered how much these shows affected some of the people I met. Being the lone motorcycle rider from California, it seemed like everyone wanted to talk to me, ask questions, and frequently offer things like food or even a place to stay.

Now, I was heading to the annual national run for my motorcycle club, the Hangmen, this year in Oklahoma. My intent was to stay on two lane roads as much as possible. Bypassing the busy, impersonal interstate with its huge truck stops, and fast food and chain restaurants and motels.

I wanted to see American again up close and personal, the way it used to be before the interstates bypassed the struggling, locally owned cafes, and motels. The way it was when I traveled alone on my chopper in the past.

Back then I did not stay in motels. I couldn't afford it. I carried a sleeping bag and slept on the ground. No tent, just a couple of Army ponchos in case of rain. I rarely went to cafes either. Dining usually consisted of cans of Campbell's pork and beans or Dinty Moore beef stew heated over an open fire if you were lucky. But I was eighteen when I left in April of 1970, young and tough.

My 1951 Pan-Head in 1970.

For this trip in 2021, even though I carried camping gear, its use was only intended for emergencies. I preferred not to try to rest my aging bones on the ground if I could help it. And besides, now I could afford a motel.

It doesn't get any better... And it didn't.

Just short of the town of Heber, Arizona, traffic came to a standstill on the narrow two-lane road.

Thinking there was an accident, everybody turned off their motors and waited patiently to get moving again. Traffic was still traveling westbound on 260, so it appeared the road was open in at least one direction.

After a half hour of waiting, wearing my armored motorcycle jacket under my leather vest, I was no longer happy with the temperature. The driver of a semi-truck offered me a bottle of cold water. I gratefully accepted.

The westbound traffic got so heavy; it came to a complete stop. Eastbound travelers shouted questions, "What's going on up there?" "Is the road open?"

A guy in a pickup truck said, "There is a forest fire, nobody is getting through, all of these cars were eastbound and have turned around."
Okay, change of plans. I had passed a little old gas station and convenience store a few miles back. The small tank on my bike always wanted

gas because the big motor with the Mikuni carburetor loved to suck it down.

During a break in the westbound traffic, I fired up the bike, made a U-turn, and headed back.

After filling the ever-thirsty tank, I walked into the little store to see what they had to eat. Wishing I had stopped in Payson for lunch, but I had been having too much fun and except coffee, had not yet eaten anything all day.

They'd been cleaned out of food because of the backup, there were no hot dogs or sandwiches left. All I could find was a can of Vienna Sausages, so along with a bottle of water, that would have to do.

Fueled and fed, I unfolded my old school paper map and looked for an alternate route. A guy who looked like a county road worker walked by and said, "Nice bike."

"Thanks," I said. "Have you heard how long they think the highway will be closed?"
"We've been here for three hours; our boss is sitting up near the front of the traffic jam. He says they anticipate another five hours."

That was not what I wanted to hear.
He asked, "Where are you heading?"

"I was hoping to make Springerville for the night."

With a frown, the guy shook his head and said, "Good luck," and turned to head back to his truck and co-workers.

It was four-thirty in the afternoon, and only two more hours to Springerville. But if the road was closed for five more hours, it would be well past eleven before I got there. I try to avoid riding at night, especially in the mountains where deer and elk seem to make a hobby out of testing your braking ability. At night they will appear out of nowhere and life can get exciting real fast.

I was unwilling to go back to Payson and find a room for the night. It was only two hours from home, and I felt that was unacceptable.

If I rode back to Strawberry and used Hwy 87 north to Winslow, I could get on Interstate 40 and head east to Holbrook and take Hwy 180 southeast to St. John, then 191 to Springerville.

Going up to the interstate would be a minimum of five hours with gas stops, maybe more. Or I could wait where I was and hope the road would open in less than five hours.

Either way, I would be riding in the dark.

Rather than sit and do nothing, I decided to back-track to Strawberry and head north on 87. With a tank full of gas, and a gourmet lunch of Vienna Sausages, I saddled up and retraced my steps westbound into a headwind and the afternoon sun, along with the rest of the refugees from the fire blockade.

One hour and sixty-two miles later, knowing gas stations toward Winslow were all but non-existent, I pulled into the same gas station where I had gotten gas earlier in the day.

After filling up, I heard an ADOT (Arizona Department of Transportation) alert from the app on my phone. When I checked it, the message was that the fire was under control, and Hwy 260 was open again.
I had just ridden an hour in the wrong direction for nothing. It was an hour later, and I was now three hours from my destination for the night.

Taking a deep breath, I set off once again, riding the same stretch of road for the third time that day, determined to get to Springerville, Arizona for the night. I had turned an easy five-hour ride into an eight-hour ride.

In the town of Star Valley, the traffic came to a complete halt for the second time that day. It was an accident. Two cars and their drivers made an unexpected and unwanted acquaintance when one of them made a careless left turn.

Once again, I shut down the motor and sat on the bike in the hot sun with my riding gear on, trying to be patient while thinking about how my schedule was getting further and further behind.

And I thought about this ride, and the past. I was heading halfway across the country. My club was celebrating its sixty-first anniversary and the fifty-year anniversary of our first annual run.

Times have changed. Being "Old school," today I am riding my stripped-down chopper with some camping gear packed aboard. It didn't matter if I needed it, what mattered is that I had something to lean back on.

Like sitting back in your easy chair in your living room. It was a concept we discovered in the early 70's. We rode long distance a lot, and it made sense to be reasonably comfortable. So, we designed our bikes with pull back handlebars and usually something for a backrest.

It might be a sleeping bag, which was always handy, or it might be between the legs of a lovely young lady.

Relaxing as you rode the long miles, it was hard to decide which was more enjoyable, the motorcycle, or your traveling companion that you melted into as you motored down the road.

That was the norm, and that was a long time ago. On this trip I was not packing anyone. No one else to talk to, no one else to worry about.

I was riding alone. The way I had done for so many years. Despite being part of a club, it was the way I preferred.

After thirty minutes the police, EMTs and firemen got the drivers off to the hospital and the cars cleared from the roadway.

I was eastbound again and seeing a lot of familiar countryside. Having ridden more than an hour since my last gas stop, I passed through the town of Heber, but did not stop at the first station I saw.

There were signs that said Overgaard, so I assumed if the town was big enough to have a sign, it was big enough to have gas.

That was a mistake. I saw no more gas stations and soon I was riding out of town into open countryside. I should have turned around and gone back to Heber, but I stubbornly pressed on, hoping to get lucky with a gas station in the middle of nowhere.

The trip meter on my little speedometer, which I reset each time I got gas, read sixty-four miles when I passed a sign saying, "Show Low, thirty-six miles."

My gas tank has a plastic tube on the side that shows the level. It is very basic, and it doesn't lie. That is when I should have turned around, but I held my breath and kept going.

With a three, point two gallon tank and a thirsty engine that usually gets thirty-two miles per gallon, I kept doing the math in my head. I **should** be able to go one-hundred and two miles, but **maybe** there will be a gas station before Show Low.

This stretch felt like the longest portion of the day's ride. I slowed down, trying to conserve fuel. I had actually thought about bringing extra gas with me but rejected the idea because storage on the bike was minimal, and besides, I'd thought it was more adventurous this way.

Suddenly that didn't seem to be such a good idea.

Sometimes, adventure is better in retrospect. Like war for example. Thinking about it later, and telling a story, it is exciting. Often in the middle of an adventure there can be a lot of doubt, and fear.

After an eternity, I entered the outskirts of Show Low, seeing civilization on either side of the road, I could no longer see gas in the tube. At the intersection where Hwy 260 turns left and merges with Hwy 60, there was a big Circle K gas station. Patting the side of the gas tank, I said, "Nice going Baby."

My trip meter read one-hundred and one miles, and the tank took two point nine gallons. I had three-tenths of a gallon left and the bike had gotten thirty-five miles per gallon. Slowing down, the high altitude and a tail wind all helped me to make it.

"Better Lucky Than Good," they say.

I didn't take time to find something to eat, I was already going to be riding in the dark and wanted to keep moving.

There are two ways to get to Springerville from Show Low. One is the scenic route on Hwy 260, with lots of mountains and curves, a beautiful ride I had done before.
That would take an hour and ten minutes. At this time of day, it would also possibly have deer and elk on the road, challenging you for the right of way.
The other way was Highway 60. Not as scenic, still two lanes, but straighter, faster, and safer. I was way behind schedule, I took Hwy 60.

Riding into the darkening evening with the sunset in my rear-view mirror, there was a combination of deep blue twilight and orange clouds ahead. Out of the forests now, the narrow road wound through rolling hills with open grasslands on both sides.

Highway 60, eastern Arizona

In Springerville, after checking into a motel at almost nine o'clock, I had been lucky to find a Mexican restaurant that was still open. Ten minutes before they closed, they were nice enough to serve me, and the taco platter was excellent. Especially since it was the only real food I'd had all day.

I was disappointed that the bar was closed, so no beer to go with the tacos. I knew there was a Safeway market in town that sold alcohol, so after shoveling down the food and leaving a good tip, I walked back down the deserted street to the motel.

Hopping on my bike, I headed to the store before it closed to buy a bottle of vodka and a quart of orange juice.

In my room, with the help of the ice machine down the sidewalk, I could enjoy a couple of drinks to help me relax after a longer day than I had anticipated.

Never turning on the television, I managed to write a few emails to let some people know I was alive and okay.

In the sixties and seventies, I traveled tens of thousands of miles by motorcycle, and I only remember getting a motel room once. It was in the town of Clovis, California on Highway 99 and I had a young lady with me. Late at night in the month of March we were riding through the San Joaquin Valley in a freezing fog, with ice building up on the front of the bike.

I needed to get back to Modesto for a court appearance at noon the next day, but at a gas stop, across the street we saw a neon sign glowing through the fog that said MOTEL, and another that said VACANCY. I had very little money, but the price of the room was only eight dollars.

After rolling the bike inside the room, we took a hot shower together. It was heavenly.

Back then, I mostly traveled alone. Out there on my own, in the wind. Riding, wandering, living my life. I never phoned home. I didn't have one. The people I knew, knew I was gone. For weeks, for months... perhaps forever.

In my room in Springerville, Arizona, I was finally able to relax. I shut down my tablet, and the rest of the world, and got some sleep.

Day 2

New Mexico

After the daily ritual of repacking the bike, and not wanting to repeat the long ride with little food from the previous day, I rode to the Mexican cafe where I'd eaten the night before and had breakfast.

I pulled up in front of the glass windows, put down the kickstand, and ignored the stares from the other patrons in the parking lot and inside the cafe. I walked in and grabbed a booth in front so I could look out and see the bike.

Lots of coffee along with a steaming plate of Huevos Rancheros really hit the spot.

Not long after leaving Springerville, I crossed the border into New Mexico, with its enormous expanses of open spaces and nothingness.

Part of that nothingness meant no towns, few towns, or very small towns, and very few gas stations.

Pie Town, New Mexico

On an old school bike, with a tank that is way too small, it tends to cause major amounts of stress like I had just gone through the day before.

Running out of gas provides its own problems. The biggest of which is sitting by the side of the road, having to admit, "Yes, I'm an idiot. I didn't get gas when I should have, and now I need your help, please, bail me out of my own stupidity."

That is how I felt about having to ask for help if things didn't work out. At the very least… "I am riding a motorcycle with a gas tank that is way too small to do this sort of thing."

But in the sense of adventure, I refused to carry any extra gas with me. I had never done it in the old days, so why now?

The towns in western New Mexico were close enough, and I was lucky enough, that I never had to go into that 'stranded biker' mode and hope people would help me.

Those personal interactions are where the best stories come from. But I've never been good at the personal interactions, so, I prefer to not run out of gas.

The wide-open spaces in New Mexico are impressive to say the least. Going through tiny town after tiny town, places like Quemado, Pie Town and Datil, I was lucky to find gas when I needed it.

Quaint places where forgotten people make a living every day, while the rest of the world passes them by, and I imagine, they are totally okay with that.

I was amazed to find, in the middle of nowhere, an enormous project, searching in outer space for alien intelligence.

Huge radio telescopes pointed skyward, into the solar system and the universe, endlessly listening for a response to our queries.

Like Pink Floyd said… "Is there anybody out there?"

Dozens of them. The VLA, which stands for 'Very Large Array' of huge radio telescopes. Listening to space, hoping for an answer to our questions. It is part of SETI, the Search for Extra Terrestrial Intelligence.

"To E.T. if you hear us… Phone home." (Please, your phone bill is due).

It was fascinating. I stopped and took several pictures. After all, if we taxpayers could spend all this money to fund the research to find ET, the least I could do is take pictures and post them on Facebook. Isn't that what it's all about?

New Mexico is quite a state when it comes to science and space. You have the Sandia Laboratories, and Los Alamos, home of the atomic bomb. Plus, White Sands missile range, Alamogordo test range and of course, Roswell, home of the captured aliens and crashed spaceships.

And more seriously, Spaceport America, just north of Las Cruces, with private companies like Virgin Galactic launching rockets into space.

The VLA, Hwy 60, New Mexico

After the VLA, I stopped in the small town of Magdalena, NM for gas. It was like so many locations I traveled through, so quaint, so small, so empty with lots of sad charm.

You wonder what it was like in its heyday. Or did it ever have a heyday.

I rode the chopper down Hwy 60, leaning back comfortably, enjoying the tailwind, wondering about aliens as I approached the big city of

Socorro, where the University of New Mexico is located.

It was getting hotter, Socorro is in the Rio Grande River valley, and it felt like I was in the desert again. Riding through town, I was tempted to stop for lunch but instead I focused on finding Interstate 25 and heading northbound.

Turning north on Interstate 25, I picked up the pace to 80 MPH for twenty-six miles until I found the junction of highway 60. I was happy to get off the hectic, high speed interstate artery and turned eastbound again.

The road turned long, straight, and lonely, with almost no one on it. I preferred it that way. As long as I did not need any help.

Not having seen any gas stations on I-25, I was now heading once again into unknown territory, which is normally a good thing, but I didn't know when I would find more gas.

The signs said the next town was Mountainair. I was learning that if a town was big enough to have a sign telling you how far it was, it probably had gas.

And it did, just one station, the rest of the town was a collection of shuttered store fronts. Businesses long since closed. It had that ghost town feel that I was to see repeatedly in back road America.

People still lived there; it was not quite a ghost town. Just a bad place to try to run a business it seemed.

Off I went, eastbound again on Hwy 60, a narrow ribbon of asphalt with no shoulder. The only things lining the road were sagebrush and the occasional cattle.

Towns were few and far between, so small that there were no gas stations. With my small tank, I was becoming obsessed with finding gas stations.

You may not even call them towns, more like communities. Little collections of homes, quiet, peaceful, half deserted locations, with names like Willard, Lucy, and Encino.
I couldn't help but wonder, where do these people fill their tanks?

Riding these long stretches of highway, sometimes straight, sometimes curving, frequently my only company were long lumbering freight trains going in one direction or the other.

I would look to see the engineers in the cab of the locomotive. Riding our bikes in the 60's, we used to wave at them, and they would hit their air horn. Sometimes I waved, but they never waved back, and never sounded the horn.

After six hours and two-hundred and eighty-six miles of riding, a nice easy day, I pulled into the town of Vaughn, New Mexico. It not only had gas, but motels.

After a swing through town to check out where I could eat, I pulled into the Bel Air Motel and checked into a room. It was nestled between Hwy 60 and the railroad tracks, so I could hear those trains that I had been waving at all day.

Asking the proprietor which restaurants were the best, he told me that Pedro's Burritos was good, but it was closed because of Covid.

Penny's Diner was good too, but they only did take out and they closed at six. It was now seven. That was everything in town.

I unloaded my gear off the bike and rode to the nearby Conoco station since they had a convenience store, hoping to find hot dogs or hamburgers.

They did not have hot food, so I looked for Beefaroni or Spaghetti O's, but they had none. In the cooler I found a pound of smoked turkey breast and some sliced cheddar cheese. That would have to do.

I bought more orange juice to go with the vodka from the night before and had a fine feast in my room. Eating cheese wrapped turkey breast with a screwdriver chaser, I was a happy camper. Especially since I got to camp indoors.

As the night progressed, the volume of Mariachi music from my new neighbors seemed to get louder, along with the volume of the Spanish language being spoken all down the line of rooms. It was Friday night and most of my new neighbors were drinking beer and probably tequila. It sounded like they were enjoying themselves, and I can relate to that. But I kept thinking about my vulnerable mode of transportation, sitting in front of my room, all by itself.

The Mexican border was just a hop, skip and a jump to the south, and I know the border guards never ask questions when you are southbound. I felt bad for my suspicions, but I would have felt even worse to be naive and have to walk home.

I'm sure it was unnecessary, but after a couple of drinks, I decided that my girl would be far happier in my room than sitting out there in the dark, all by herself.

So, I opened the door and beckoned her to come to me. We spent the night together. We talked, we cuddled. She was happy, and so was I.

Vaughn, New Mexico

Day 3

Texas

After working for years as an airline pilot, getting up at Zero Dark Thirty, one of my little pleasures of retired life, is not having to get up early.

Despite the comforting smell of gasoline, I slept until 8:30 when I decided I needed coffee and breakfast.

After evicting my roommate for the night, I packed her back up, took the remainder of cheese and deli turkey out of the little refrigerator and had breakfast with the remainder of last night's orange juice to wash it down.

Firing up the bike is always such a satisfying sound that fills your chest with pride and gratitude. To hear and feel it respond to the twist of the key, the starter engages, the motor roars to life. "Thank you baby! We're going to ride again; you didn't let me down."

We rode back to the Conoco station with the convenience store, and I filled her tank. Then pulling away from the pumps, I went into the store in search of coffee. Which they had in large amounts. I bought a twenty-ounce cup and stood out by the bike, enjoying the morning ritual of a mandatory caffeine injection.

While I was there, a couple on an Electra Glide Ultra pulled up, got their gas, and then parked next to me. They were from Northern California, near Sacramento and had just been to the Big Bend area of Texas. A long trip, they had gotten their share of rain.

While I sipped the hot black coffee, we talked about how fun it was getting beat up by the wind. I empathized that they would be enjoying a lot of headwinds for the next few days. They were seasoned motorcycle travelers and were cheerfully up to the task.

I finished my coffee, and we said our goodbyes.
"Stay safe,"
"You too!"

A brief encounter of Two Wheel Warriors battling the elements. The four-wheel public cannot begin to understand.

I tossed my cup in the trash, inserted earplugs, donned my helmet, fired up the eager Ultima engine, and resumed my journey eastbound.

Making a left just out of town to stay on Hwy 60, I headed into a cloudy sky. Thankfully without the sun in my eyes, I was hoping they would not turn into rain clouds.

Highway 60 seemed to go straight for the next one hundred miles. It did not turn one degree. Or at least it seemed that way.

The next town was Fort Sumner, famous for the place where Pat Garrett killed Billy the Kid. Having just gone sixty miles, all I cared about was that they had gas.

I suspect at least fifty percent of the economy of Fort Sumner is based on the Billy the Kid legend. It is a very interesting part of old west history that should be kept alive.

The first station I came to was full of a group of bikers on baggers, so I passed it by. Not being very sociable, I didn't want to spend time standing around talking, answering all the questions… "Where are you from… Where are you going?"

One of the never-ending gas stops

So, I rode on through town looking for the next gas station.

There wasn't one.

Riding out the other side of the small town, I made a U-Turn and headed back to the Allsup's station and convenience store.

On the way back, I passed the big pack of bikes that had just left the station. Cool, no questions to answer. I pulled in and gassed up, hit their bathroom to get rid of some coffee and was back on my way. Free from unnecessary conversation.

I rode past all the Billy the Kid motels, Billy the Kid cafes, and the Billy the Kid museums without any feelings of guilt of not visiting them. I already knew the history and was happy to get out of town and down the road. Right then, that was my only goal in life.

Just a few miles out of town I was confronted with a town named for the Taliban! Why the hell would anybody in New Mexico name a town for them???

It turned out my quick reading of the map was quite wrong. It was not Taliban, it was Taiban. Named for Taiban Creek and was famous for being the place where Pat Garrett captured Billy and his buds on December 23, 1880. Okay, my bad.

I didn't slow down and headed for the big town of Clovis, New Mexico. The biggest town I'd seen in days and home to Cannon Air Force Base.

I knew there would be gas there. I was beginning to like New Mexico.

Deciding to pass on lunch, I rode out of Clovis and shortly after that, the appropriately named town of Texico, on the border of Texas and New Mexico.

Entering the state of Texas, I turned northeast, still on Hwy 60. Just before the junction of Hwy 86, I encountered the Bovina Cattle Company.

It was a giant feedlot on the right side of the highway that seemed to go on for miles but was probably not more than two. If there weren't a million cattle, it certainly smelled that way. The wind was bringing a scent so strong you could have cut it with a knife.

Just past the stockyard, at the town of Bovina, Hwy 86 ran due east. The wind was out of the south, and it was warm but not hot as long as you were moving down the road.

Dimmitt, Texas is a good-sized town which supported the oil, agriculture, and cattle industries. Plus, now giant wind turbines which seem to be everywhere in this part of the state. I kept moving. Somehow it felt normal to be hungry while riding. Thinking back to so many years ago when I traveled on little money, gas in the tank was more important than food. I tend to get a bit focused on getting down the road. Eating can wait.

My odometer and plastic tube of a gas gauge said I could make it to the next town. At the Pilot truck stop at the edge of Tulia, Texas, some real cowboys in pickup trucks, wearing cowboy hats and spurs were getting gas also.

After filling my tank, I pulled the bike to the front of the convenience store, went in and bought a bottle of water. Drinking it, I stood in the shade of the building near the front door and studied my paper map to see how long I had to go for the day.

Local folks going in and out commented about the bike or about the heat. One older gentleman said, "Hot on that back?"
Not having my hearing aids in, I said, "What?"

He repeated, "Hot on that back?"

I thought, 'The back of what, of course I ride on the back, does he mean the seat?'

He must have wondered if I spoke English, which I did, but my Texan was a little rusty.
I just said, "Yes," and he walked into the store.

Finally, it dawned on me that he was saying "Bike," but that Texas accent came out as "Back."

In the 90's Texas had an ad campaign for tourism where they said,
"It's like a whole 'nother country."

I thought, 'They've got that right, a foreign language and all.'

They are good people though, like all of middle America.

I didn't stop in Quitaque, which they pronounce "Kitty Kway," according to a sign at the edge of town and they claim to be the Bison Capital of Texas. With a population of a little over four hundred people, they may have more buffalo than humans. The town was not big enough to have a gas station.

An hour after Tulia, I was pulling into Turkey, Texas. My destination for the night.

Turkey is just south of Caprock Canyon State Park and the Palo Duro Canyon which they call the Grand Canyon of Texas. It is the second largest canyon in the United States.

Pulling into town on now familiar deserted streets, I hung a left and a block off the main drag, and found the Hotel Turkey, the only game in town for a room.

There was no one in the lobby. Hearing music, I followed a hallway towards the back of the hotel, my boots clumping on the old wooden floor.

I was amazed when I walked onto the large patio to find it packed with people sitting at tables. A live band was playing, and waitresses were running around serving patrons. So much for ghost towns.

It looked like people had come from miles around to be here, having more the look of tourists than locals.

I sat at an open table and ordered a beer from the first waitress that came by and inquired as to who was running the front desk.

Hotel Turkey

The beer arrived first, nice and cold, then the lady who ran the hotel.

I inquired about a room, and she told me they were full up. Oh no, who'd have thought this old place in the middle of nowhere would be so popular, but it was Saturday night after all.

"How far is the next town with a hotel?"

"Which way?"

"Eastbound."

"That'll be Childress."

"How far is that?"

"Just under an hour, but there is a guy who has been renovating the offices of an old lumber mill into guest rooms. It's just across main street, he may have a room open, I can check on that if you like."

"Please do, I'd rather not ride another hour today. I'll be right here getting something to eat."

I was just digging into the hamburger when she came back with good news. "He's got a room for ya, but it'll be an hour before it is ready if that's okay."

"That's great, I'll hang out here, just let me know."
Behind the hotel patio was a large yard of mowed grass with a picnic table under an oak tree.

Finishing my hamburger, I ordered another beer and waited in the shade of that tree to get away from the noisy crowd and the too loud band.

I don't like to make reservations when traveling by motorcycle. There are too many things that can keep you from arriving on time, weather, breakdowns, road closures due to fires, or accidents. I like to wing it, and most of the time it works out. This was one of those times.

The room was new and clean and comfortable, it even had Wi-Fi.

Unloading the bike, I made myself at home and took a shower. Stretching out on the king-sized bed felt great. After answering a couple of emails, I slept like a rock.

Day 4

Wichita Falls

It was Sunday morning in Turkey, Texas and the streets looked like a ghost-town again.

As I pulled out onto Main Street, the only cars in sight were parked.

I turned on my GoPro and started recording. The setting reminded me of that sad Johnny Cash song, written by Kris Kristofferson, "Sunday Mornin' Comin' Down."

I had always liked it for the sense of loneliness it so accurately portrays, so the lyrics started going through my head as I rode. Only right now, I wasn't wishing "Lord that I was stoned."

I was wishing that I had some coffee.

I also wanted to get going, with high hopes that the bike would keep running as well as it had been, and it would be nice if I didn't get rained on.

I had an appointment in Wichita Falls.

The only breakfast in Turkey would be at the Hotel Turkey, but the night before they had told me they would not open until ten o'clock. I could be a whole bunch of miles away by then.

On Main Street, I passed two small museums on the left side of the road. One, a very old gas station, the first Phillips 66 in all of Texas, built in 1928. It didn't have gas.

Right next to it is a museum for the late country singer Bob Wills. His old bus that he and his band traveled in, is parked next to the tiny building, which was not much bigger than the bus.

Hwy 86 turned left at 9th Street where the only gas station in town was.

I was happy to find it was open. Because I would not be going anywhere if it was not.

Riding out of town, eastbound on Hwy 86, I was surprised at how green it got, often with thick tangled growth lining both sides of the road.

The evening before, I had asked one of the waitresses why the town was named Turkey? She said, "Because of all of the Rio Grande sub-species of wild turkeys in the area."

I said, "Well, that makes sense."

It got more humid as the morning went on. The clouds in the buttermilk sky seemed to be threatening rain, but eventually cleared into an azure blue and the sun got hotter as I went east.

There was not a single town or even a farmhouse for thirty miles, until I came to civilization again at Estelline, where Hwy 86 dead ends into Texas State Hwy 287.

Estelline had a Baptist Church, a liquor store, and a Post Office and, from what I could see, nothing else but houses. I made a right and merged with the trucks and the traffic.

I said goodbye to the quiet two-lane roads for a while. Hwy 287 is a four-lane divided highway, much like an interstate, except it goes through the middle of towns, much as the interstates used to before they built the bypasses.

After riding for an hour, I came into Childress. Seeing a restaurant that advertised breakfast, I hit the brakes and pulled in.

Always happy to relax, sit still and stop vibrating for a while, I plopped into a booth and ordered coffee, ham, and eggs over easy and hash-browns.

One of the restaurant employees had been eyeing me since I came in. Finally, he came over to my table and told me how much he liked my bike. He asked a lot of questions about it, then he said he had a Harley Davidson, Soft Tail and showed me a picture of it on his phone.

I thought he was Native American but was surprised when he mentioned "coming to this country."

I asked, "Where are you from?"

He said, "Nepal."

"Really? Wow! Where abouts, Kathmandu?"

He said, "Yes."

"I always wanted to go there. It looks like a wonderful place, and here you are in Texas riding a Harley! How cool is that!"

I offered him to sit at my table and we chatted about motorcycles while I ate. He was a nice guy and wanted to hear about my trip. I gave him the rundown so far, and he told me about Nepal.

Before I took off, he came outside and we did a selfie together and wished each other, "Good luck, stay safe."

Continuing southeast on 287, I passed through several small towns including Quanah, which is named after the half-white, half-Comanche Warrior, Quanah Parker.

He was the son of Cynthia Ann Parker, who was kidnapped at ten years old and raised as a Comanche. When he grew up, he led uprisings against the white invasion and became the last chief of the Comanche tribe.

Eventually he agreed to peace and helped to put his people onto a reservation in Oklahoma. It is well known state history in Texas.

Quanah, Texas

On the way out of town I passed an old restaurant, so I stopped to take a picture. In Google Maps you can see it was still operating in 2019, but now, like so many small businesses around the country, it is shut down.

The next couple of hours on the super slab of four lane concrete flew by, except for gas stops which were plentiful and easy to find.

Wichita Falls was the first real city on my trip, so I had to know where I was going. I was not using a Garmin or even my phone for navigation. I knew how, but I didn't feel it went along with the spirit of this journey. The whole old school thing and all.

I had to stop a couple of times to get oriented and memorized the streets that would take me to my destination.

Only running slightly late, I was able to make my way to where I needed to be.

Finally motoring slowly down the quiet residential street, I turned into a green yard under a giant oak tree and shut the faithful Ol' Girl down.

My son Chris walked out of the garage, I got off the bike and we gave each other a big hug.

He had ridden his motorcycle down from Edmond, Oklahoma to meet up with me. Staying at a friend's house in Wichita Falls, we were going to spend the night and continue to the Hangmen run in the morning.

Even though the bike was running fine, with the hot temperatures, the thought had been nagging at me that I had not done an oil change before leaving Arizona.

After a brief discussion, we jumped in his brother's pick-up truck and headed off to an auto parts store to get supplies.

While the oil change was in progress, someone had the brilliant idea to go to the Eskimo Hut where they had a drive-through that served frozen mango daiquiris to go. Gotta love Texas.

You could order how many shots of rum you wanted in them. The maximum was ten, so that is what we got.

Chris and I, with refreshments, Texas style

Despite the refreshments, I managed to get my oil changed.

We had a fun evening hanging out with Chris's friends, including his brother Rick and John, the Mayor of Texas, (It's a long story), and his wife Cathy.

After an awesome dinner of ribs and BBQ, we spent the rest of the night sitting in the back yard, talking and laughing at our buddy Jared's funny stories.

Watching lightning and listening to the thunder for hours was great.

It just wouldn't seem like Texas without thunder.

Day 5

Oklahoma

The guest bed I slept in was perfect. It was so comfortable, I wished I could buy it and ship it home. Or maybe it was just fatigue.

Our friends were starting their day while Chris and I drank coffee from a Keurig machine and packed our bikes.

Leaving Wichita Falls

It was Monday and the day was already humid, although not yet hot.

We were in no hurry, having all day to go two-hundred and twenty-five miles. I wanted to give the morning rush hour traffic in the city time to dissipate before we hit the road.

By ten o'clock we were making our first gas stop outside town as we picked up Hwy 79 to head northeast.

Chris was riding his 1999 Harley Davidson Soft Tail. A sharp looking black and chrome classic that used to be mine for ten years. It now had a six-speed transmission and cruised the highways and interstates as fast as any newer model. The eighty-inch Evo motor was more than adequate because the bike is so light.

Riding with their son is something that many motorcycle riders have enjoyed, but it was particularly special to me.

Because of the wild days of my biker lifestyle, and decisions I made back in the seventies, I had not been part of his life for forty-three years.

It was not the way I wanted it, but after splitting up with his mother, she did not want me to be part of his life. I lost track of them after both she and I moved around.

Fortunately, in 2016, he found me online and we've had a great relationship ever since. AND he rides motorcycles. Must be something in the genes. Or the jeans.

We ride well together, like we had done it all our lives. Today, he took the lead because he knew where we were going. Soon after leaving Wichita Falls, we were in Oklahoma, sticking to the two-lane roads as much as possible. He likes to do that too.

I frequently had to keep reminding myself, hey, you are actually riding motorcycles with your son! And I would look over at him on his bike, just to confirm that it was really happening.

It got hotter as the roads wound through rural Oklahoma, lush, green, and humid.

Hwy 79 turned into Hwy 70 through Waurika and then Ardmore where we stopped for lunch at the Two Frogs Grill and relaxed for a while in air-conditioned comfort.

In the dimly lit, friendly atmosphere of the restaurant, over a lunch of hamburgers and iced tea, Chris said, "Ya know, this is like one of the high points in my life."

Almost overcome with emotion, I swallowed hard and said, "Mine too. For years I longed just to find you, and never dared to hope that it could be this good."

Breaking the mood of the moment before it got too mushy, Chris laughed and said, "Well, good thing we've lived this long then."

I said, "Yeah, good thing." And dug into my cheeseburger.

Soon we were back out in the heat riding through small towns, farmland, forests and then small towns again.

Continuing to stop about once an hour because of my small tank, Chris did not need to worry about running out of gas while riding with me.

Finally, we found Hwy 69 and turned northeast, through towns like Atoka, Kiowa, and McAlester.

After six hours on the road, including the lunch stop, we came to Arrowhead State Park in Canadian, Oklahoma where the 2021 Hangmen MC run was being held.

Riding around the whole park, we stopped into the office to get directions. Chris and I finally found the Harbin Barracks, nestled back in the trees away from the main road.

We pulled in and parked among all the other bikes from around the country and shut down. We greeted brothers we had not seen in months, or some, since the annual run last year.

Chris already knew almost everybody. This was not his first Hangmen run. Cold beers were shoved into our hands, and we joined the party already in progress.

Before it got too late, we pulled our bikes over to one of the many barracks' and unloaded our gear. Claiming our territory by picking a bunk, we then went back to the party.

The talk ranged from travel experiences to motorcycles and plans for the week. How was the ride? How was the weather? Who broke down? Who crashed? who wasn't here yet?

It was always good to see brothers from around the country. It was good to be where you were going, you could relax for a while.

The bike got you there, which is always a good feeling. Having a dependable bike is like having a dependable woman, comforting and worry free.

It doesn't get any better than this.

Harbin Barracks, Arrowhead State Park, Canadian, Oklahoma

Harbin Barracks I was told, used to be a military base. It consisted of scattered buildings with bunk rooms, wide expanses of neatly mowed lawns and huge oak trees.

There was a central building with a large dining area, a kitchen with a walk-in refrigerator, and a freezer. Other buildings held bathrooms and showers.

At night, the whole area was well lit. It was a beautiful spot, but in June, it was miserably humid all day and all night. Living in Arizona for the last two decades, I am used to a dry heat.

We had the whole area to ourselves, having rented it for five days.

Indoors, the air conditioning was running 24/7 and due to the humid air, while inside, to me it was freezing cold. When I would walk out into the humidity, my glasses would fog up.

The Oklahoma crew was hosting the run. Prospects and other members from around the country helped also. They all did a great job.

Taking charge, they cooked meals every morning and evening, providing refreshments, including water, soda, beer, and moonshine.

And since it was legal, pot for those who wanted it.

Just after ten o'clock we got a call from Tray, the Phoenix Hangmen chapter president.

Tray said, "Hey, we need some help out here, can someone send a truck with a trailer to pick up some bikes?"

"Yeah, sure, where are you? What happened?"

"Near Eufaula just off highway 69, Juan and Bubba crashed hard after hitting a pothole."

"What? That must have been a hell of a pothole!

"Yeah, it was, they both hit it."

"How are they doing?"

"Juan's hurt bad, he has multiple compound fractures. Ringo has been putting his medical training from the Marine Corps to work, probably saved his life. The EMT's are loading him into an ambulance now."

"How about Bubba?"

"He's okay, just bruises it looks like, he's up and walking, but both bikes are a mess, we need someone to come and get them."

We were bummed by the bad news, but happy that everyone was still breathing and had a pulse. Trucks and trailers were dispatched to bring in the broken bikes, others headed to the hospital to try to help.

Another day in the life. There are always risks when you ride motorcycles. At least we weren't commuting on a busy freeway every day where people lose their lives at an alarming rate.

Or die from a virus. We were living free! Riding and partying with our brothers. Living the life we chose.

Chris and I stayed up to wait for more news from the rest of the Phoenix chapter guys when they finally rode in.

There was an endless supply of cold beer, whiskey, and moonshine, which I had learned the hard way to avoid. Moonshine likes to sneak up on you.

I wandered around the camp, visiting with people, talking, laughing and drinking, it's always that way on the first night.

It's hard to pack it in, even after having ridden for hours earlier in the day. I finally called it quits at 3:30 AM and Chris was still going.

Staggering into our barracks and finding my bunk, after the oppressive heat and humidity, even at night, the air conditioning in the bunk rooms felt freezing cold.

I pulled my sleeping bag from its sack, took off my boots, and climbed into it. Ironic to be so hot outside, and here I was huddled in a sleeping bag.

After hours of standing around talking with people, laying down flat and not moving felt like heaven.

I thought, is this what it feels like when you die? Finally able to rest?

Who knows...? I happily drifted off to sleep.

Juan's motorcycle. Note the bent rim. The pothole was fixed the next day.

Days 6 through 8
The Run

The next four days were kind of a blur, which is normal at a national run.

We had events like a club ride to the Arkansas border, to a BBQ place that wanted to put on a feed just for us. We had an auction with lots of laughter from the friendly rivalry where people tried to out-bid each other.

One night we had a live band set up outside under the oak trees, playing until ten o'clock when the park rules said they had to quit.

It's always good to see new members who will bring this club into the future. For me, it is also great to see people that I have known for over fifty years.

An old buddy of mine named Paul lives in Georgia. We had met when I lived in Alaska for a while in the seventies and was trying to get a job on the pipeline.
He was never a biker but always loved to ride. We had stayed in touch ever since but lived on opposite sides of the country.

He was on a trip out west on his motorcycle with some friends and was in the neighborhood.

Well, he was in Cheyenne, Wyoming, almost nine-hundred miles away, close enough. We had not seen each other in a while, and he wanted to stop by.

Thursday afternoon he showed up and we had a great time visiting. He enjoyed meeting the guys from the club and they liked him and his unusual Tilting Motors motorcycle conversion.

Thursday evening was 'steak night' and I made sure to give the guys a hard time for eating so well on a run.

Back in the sixties and seventies, we bought our dinner at the last gas stop of the day. Usually, we got canned goods or maybe hot dogs.

Anything that you could cook over an open fire. It could be hard to pack the hot dog buns on a bike without squashing them though.
All too soon, it was over, Friday morning, everyone was heading out.

Day 9

On to Edmond

After another late night, I awoke to the familiar sound of motorcycles starting up. People leaving early to beat the heat. I raised my head to look around the bunk room and saw that Chris and Paul were still sleeping. So, I laid my head down and closed my eyes again.

It was already hot and humid by the time Chris and I packed up the bikes. We were going to Chris's house in Edmond, Oklahoma. Once again, staying off the interstate, it would be an easy day of only one-hundred and fifty miles.

Paul had left his buddies in Cheyenne and did not have to be back home yet. Having known each other for forty-five years, we had never ridden together so he decided to come with us.

We pulled the bikes to the center of the campground near the cabin with the dining room and kitchen. It had become the gathering place for everybody for the last five days. The kitchen had been shut down and packed up, there would be no breakfast or coffee today.

After making the rounds and saying goodbye, we finally rode out to Hwy 69 and turned north.

Fifteen minutes up the road in Eufaula, we spotted a diner and pulled in for a late breakfast. Relaxing in the air conditioning we gulped hot black coffee with the food.

Leaving Eufaula, we picked up Hwy 9 westbound. Chris and I took turns in the lead, with Paul bringing up the rear. OK 9 was narrow with no shoulder most of the way. The forests and crops on either side were lush green. Occasionally we would see old farmhouses along the road, sometimes occupied, sometimes abandoned.

We kept a wary eye on the sky, watching for thunderstorms, but luckily none appeared.

In the town of Seminole, the road opened up to four lanes with a grassy median. It was Friday afternoon and there was a lot of traffic.

I was leading and made the mistake of bypassing several gas stations because they were not convenient to get into, thinking I would find something better. Then we ended up heading out of town where Hwy 9 merged with Hwy 270 and went back to two lanes.

Leaving Seminole and its gas stations behind us I was sweating it until we finally came to a Sinclair station in the small town of Earlsboro. Eighty-three miles on my little tank and of course, I was the only one running low.

We filled our tanks and bought bottles of cold water and guzzled them down, trying to stay hydrated.

At Tecumseh, Hwy 270 turned north and merged with Hwy 177. I was in front when I looked in my rearview mirror and saw Chris pull over to the side of the road and stop.

When it was safe, I did a U-turn and went back to find his foot shifter had fallen off.

Fortunately, Paul, riding in back had seen it come off and bounce into the grass at the shoulder and was able to find it.

A few minutes with a tool kit, and emergency repairs by the side of the road were complete. Chris was ready to ride again.

Just past Shawnee we crossed under Interstate 40 and kept going north on 177, looking for old Route 66.

We missed that turn and ended up going another twenty miles to the town of Perkins before we figured out our mistake. Stopping at a gas station, we were entertained by a guy who wanted to talk about the motorcycles while we drank more water, and I studied my map.

Riding back southbound, we found Old 66 and turned west. It is always an interesting ride on original sections of Route 66 anywhere in the country.

Old homes and businesses are everywhere. The road was completed in 1926, so some of these buildings can be as much as one hundred years old. Many of them are abandoned, but many still operating.

Normally I like riding sections of Old 66, but it wasn't long before I decided that this section of highway was the worst piece of road I had ridden on this whole trip.

It felt like it had seams about every ten feet that were like mini speed bumps.

Even though my Ultima chopper has a swing-arm rear suspension like a Harley Soft Tail, you would not know it. The ride is rough, and each seam had me swearing with pain and I thought it would never stop.

The state of Oklahoma has neglected this road for too long. Certainly modern cars and trucks, even modern motorcycle suspensions, deal with this rotten piece of road better than my low riding bike.

With all the roads I had ridden on in two weeks, and some of them were bad, this one stood out as the worst.

At least this portion of Route 66 led straight into Edmond and turned into West Edmond Road, just a couple blocks from my son's house.

Five hours after leaving the state park and the run, we pulled into Chris's driveway.

We had used an hour for lunch and another hour for the mistaken detour.

It was great to get off the bikes for the day, sit in the folding chairs in his backyard and drink cold beers in the shade of the trees.

Hearing we were back, some friends came over and wanted to hear all about the trip. Paul, seems to be comfortable in any group or environment, he kept people entertained with jokes, conversation and stories.

We talked late into the night, then Paul made a hotel reservation, since Chris already had a house full of guests. Saying our goodbyes, he rode off into the night and would be eastbound early in the morning.

Always finding something to talk about, Chris and I stayed up until the wee hours before I finally called it quits and I headed for the guest room.

After all the riding, visiting, and partying of the last ten days, I was looking forward to a little down time.

Paul on his Tilting Motors/Harley Conversion

Days 10 through 12

It is always nice to get a chance to relax and hang out with my son and his family and we made the most of it.

I had planned to be on the road Sunday the 20th, but that turned out to be Father's Day. Chris and I had never spent a Father's Day together, so obviously I had to stay one more day.

We shopped together, and cooked some great meals, and did a little drinking too.

We had a wonderful time and I made plans to leave Monday.

But in the morning, there was a line of thunderstorms coming in from the west. I decided to delay my departure until they passed.

It rained hard until mid-afternoon, so Chris and I went to lunch at a one of my favorite gourmet diners, the Waffle House.

But they could only do take-out because they did not have enough employees since the government has been paying people not to work.

Change of plans, we went to an International House of Pancakes, where they only had half of the tables operating for the same reason.

Next, we decided that I needed a new phone, so off we went to a Verizon store.

The only phone they had available was the twelve-hundred-dollar model. I said, thanks but no thanks.

Next, we went to a Best Buy where I got a late model phone for one quarter of that price.

By the time we ran other errands and got back to his house, the rain had stopped, but it was now getting late enough that I would be riding in the dark, so I put off my departure until Tuesday.

Chris and I headed to the grocery store to get more supplies to fix another fine dinner.

Day 13

Kansas

It was great getting to spend time with my son, his lovely wife, and my awesome grandkids, (Biased? What, me?), but I was dying to be back on the road.

After getting gas, I found my way out of town to the countryside and headed west on Hwy 33 towards Kingfisher, feeling a sense of freedom, as if I had just been let out of jail.

Obviously not a good comparison when talking about visiting family, but that is what came to mind as I rode down the highway. I felt elated; I was alone, on my own, in the wind. I had been turned loose again, just me and the bike.

Heading into unknown territory, riding roads I had never been on. It felt new and the sense of adventure rose like a young hawk spreading its wings and lifting into the air for the first time.

During a gas stop I noticed on my map that there are two small towns just to the north on road 790. The towns are called Alpha and Omega. 'The First and the Last,' (letters in the Greek alphabet). The beginning and the end.

I thought it was quite interesting to name two towns this way and I wanted to go through there and investigate, but I did not have time. And I doubt they would have appreciated my nosiness, anyway, poking around small towns without a reason to be there.

Normally I spend almost no time sight-seeing when on the road. I want to make use of the daylight and if I am lucky, the dry weather, to get where I want to be for the night.

In this case, where I wanted to be was Dodge City, which was two hundred and fifty miles and four and a half hours according to my new phone. But Google Maps does not take small gas tanks and even smaller bladders into account. Nor lunch.

I did a detour through the town of Watonga after seeing the large golden dome of the courthouse. Plus, I thought I might spot a diner or someplace to eat.
No such luck on the diner, but I did get some interesting GoPro footage of the small town as I rode through but did not stop.

Frequent gas and bathroom stops will stretch a four-and-a-half-hour trip into five and a half. Even a short, fast food stop for lunch can make that six.

I mentioned earlier about in the old days, our main sustenance while on the road was canned goods. Not just beer, but beef stew or pork and beans.

Recently some old-timers with the club started producing pictures of So.Cal. guys in the sixties or seventies eating pork and beans out of a can, alongside the road, with a Buck knife.

Back then they had not yet invented the wonderful Beefaroni. So, thinking of this as I rode along, I was unwilling to stop at a diner for an hour, or even to take less time for fast food.

In the Town of Selling when I stopped for gas, I decided to pay tribute to the old days and get pork and beans for lunch.

Walking into the mini mart store, I was delighted to see they had Beanee-Weanees. With a pull tab, no can opener needed.

I asked for a plastic spoon and suddenly, along with a large hot coffee in a paper cup, lunch was served, 1960's style.

Who needs 'Steak Night?'

Lunch stop in Selling, Oklahoma.

I was now following Hwy 270 to Fort Supply and Buffalo. Around Buffalo it was easy to imagine vast herds of buffalo roaming that broken up land.

There were many rolling hills and ravines that could hide herds of a million buffalo along with bands of Indian warriors on horses that the

American Cavalry would chase in vain. The Indians knew the land better than the soldiers.

I was not just going down the road on a motorcycle, I was experiencing a small part of the history of our land, at seventy-five miles per hour.

Motoring along on my chopper, heading west, I was fighting against the wind coming out of the south.

The long straight Kansas roads revealed the Emerald City of OZ at the end of it. Gleaming towers reaching into the sky with lush green fields lining the Yellow Brick Road.

The motor purred along like the Cowardly Lion and the valve covers clattered, sounding a little like the Tin Man.

It might have been nice to have Dorothy on the back of the bike, to lean back between her thighs. I could help her out with those flying monkeys and that bitch of a witch.

It was a nice fantasy to pass the time and the miles, but those towers at the end of the road were not the Emerald City, and the road was not yellow, just the center line.

The towers were huge grain silos, and it seemed every town in Kansas had them.

As I went from town to town, more towers would appear straight down the road, and the fantasy would start all over again.

As I headed for Dodge City, the crosswind was punching me back and forth like a giant invisible boxer.

Every semi-truck that passed in the opposite direction hit me with a wall of air that felt like getting hit by a giant tennis racket, snapping my head back for an instant.

The trucks that were hauling cattle carried behind that tennis racket, a slap in the face of barnyard odor that was almost overwhelming. Fortunately, it only lasted an instant, then like the truck, it was gone.

It was more like doing battle with the wind and the road than just riding a motorcycle.

Why Dodge City? I had never been there before, and it was in the general direction I was going, plus it held a part of the legend of Wyatt Earp. I guess you could say I'm a fan. Not of Kurt Russell or Kevin Costner, but the actual man I had read so many books about.

After a couple of wrong turns, which turned my trip for the day into a seven-hour ride. It was hot and traffic in Dodge was heavy as I arrived.

The motor on the Ultima always sounds so characteristic when you slow down to go through a town. The uneven galloping, popping, and stuttering makes it sound like it is not comfortable going slow.

Maybe it's the cams that are in it. I don't know, I did not build the motor. But it always sounds nervous and uncertain at slow speeds.

The same way I feel nervous and uncertain in strange towns.

As usual I had not made reservations, so I rode through the town, checking out hotels that looked like worthy places to stay the night.

Riding past the more expensive chain hotels, I was searching for the privately owned 'Mom and Pop' type places.

And I found one right on Wyatt Earp Boulevard. The Holiday Motel. Named after Doc Holliday? I didn't ask. It was run by a nice Chinese gentleman who did not speak good English.

He called his wife, who did better with the American lingo, and without any bargaining, I got the cheapest room of the trip for $35 for the night.

I could not say "Yes," fast enough.

I really wanted to go down to Front Street and check out the night life in the old saloons where Wyatt and Bat Masterson used to do their jobs of enforcing the law.

I wanted to drink beer at a bar where Wyatt may have stood and prop my boot upon the brass rail where maybe he had placed his.

But I was tired and wanted to find some food before I hit the sack. And I did not want to ride the bike to downtown, have a few beers and ride it back to the motel.

Doc Holliday's motel?

There was a Chinese-Sushi-Steakhouse restaurant right in front of the motel, so I opted for that.

They had Sapporo, my favorite Japanese beer, and the sushi was excellent. By the time I had eaten, I had no desire to go anywhere or do anything except bury my face in a pillow and explore dreamland.

Day 14

Gettin' outta Dodge

Every evening I would unpack the bike and bring my gear into the room. In the morning I would reverse the process. Everything had its place, and it went back together the same way every time.

Riding a couple of short blocks to the Dodge House restaurant, I pulled in for coffee and breakfast.

Having already discovered in the small towns in Kansas, diners and coffee shops seemed to be even less common than gas stations, I thought I would take advantage while I was in the big city.

While eating, I contemplated touring Front Street, the old part of town talked about in the stories of Wyatt's law enforcement career, where the action was.

There were statues and a museum, and the old buildings are preserved and still in business of one kind or another. Only now, most are not saloons and brothels like in the 1880's.

Wearing my riding gear, I felt bulky and hot, and was not in the mood to trudge around a museum.

My travel plans for the day consisted of riding two hundred and eighty-seven miles. Which according to Google maps, would take four hours and thirty-four minutes.

But that is if you are in a car or truck. On a motorcycle, especially this one, I was looking at five and a half, to six hours.

Another part of the Dodge City mystique is Gun Smoke, James Arness as United States Marshall Matt Dillon. Patterned of course after Wyatt Earp.

Even though that was a good, long running television show, Matt Dillon is a fictional character.

I was more into the reality of history. Wyatt Earp is as much a part of American history as Daniel Boone and Davey Crockett, Billy the Kid, or Wild Bill Hickok.

Dodge House restaurant on Wyatt Earp Boulevard

Leaving the Dodge House, I rode back towards the old center of town to Central Ave. Parking the bike in a lot, I walked to the big statue of Wyatt Earp on the corner.

He was a lot taller than I thought.

Seeing me taking pictures of the statue, a pretty young lady who worked for the city came over and asked, "Would you like a picture with Wyatt?"
I almost said no, but she was charming and enthusiastic with a nice smile, so I said, "Sure."

After taking the shot, she said, "Have you been to the Boot Hill Museum?"
"No, is it any good?"

"Yeah, I just went to it for the first time the other day. I learned a lot."

"Where are you from?"

"Right here in Dodge. I just got back from college and I'm settling down and just got this job."

"You like it here then?"

"Yes, I love it."

I said, "How nice, thank you for the picture," and turned to walk back to the bike.

She called out, "My pleasure, have a safe trip."

"Thank you, I'll do my best," I smiled back. Fifty years ago, I might have found an excuse to stick around.

It was already hot, and I wanted to be on the road. I would leave the Boot Hill Museum tour for some other time. It would be a good excuse to come back.

With Wyatt Earp in Dodge City. I don't think he was really that tall.

Pulling out of the parking lot, I rode across the street to the train station where there was a big sign that said, Dodge City. Parking my bike under it, I took one last picture before moving on.

Getting outta Dodge!

Turning south on 1st Avenue, I left town the way I had arrived the evening before. After crossing the Arkansas River, a couple of miles later I turned right on Hwy 400 and soon turned onto Hwy 56.

I resumed my battle against the wind out of the south and the ever-present cattle hauling trucks with their vicious blast of air and brief foul odor.

Westbound again, I was again riding in the Land of Oz, on narrow two-lane roads. Seemingly with the Emerald City, I mean tall grain silos, always in the distance, and railroad tracks alongside the road connecting those silos to wherever they took the grain.

Huge wind turbines now lined both sides of the highway as well. It was easy to see which way the wind was blowing by seeing the direction the propeller blades were facing.

I was traveling through small towns with names like Ensign, Montezuma, and Sublette, which was named after Bill Sublette. He one of the original mountain men from the Rocky Mountain Fur Company from the 1820's and 30's.

Temperatures were warm, but not too hot as long as you kept moving. I was seeing news stories online about a heat wave in the Pacific Northwest with temperatures soaring over one-hundred and ten-degrees.

I felt fortunate to be in the low to mid-nineties so far, and my plan was to stay relatively north, getting into the mountains as I headed west.

Just after Elkhart, Kansas, Hwy 56 crossed into Oklahoma and suddenly it felt hotter. Or maybe it was just because I knew I was in Oklahoma.

Hwy 56 merged into Hwy 412 as I continued southwest. After crossing into New Mexico, it just barely cut the corner of northwest Texas for about 100 feet before crossing back into New Mexico, so I guess you could say I rode through four states that day.

Pulling into the town of Clayton, New Mexico, on Main Street I found a Phillips 66 station and pulled in to gas up.

After filling the tank, I rolled the bike away from the pumps and went inside to buy a bottle of cold water.

There was a stack of pallets in front of the store, so I took off my hot leather cut and armored jacket and sat down to drink the water and study my paper map to make sure of my route. I didn't want to repeat the mistakes of wrong turns like I had done the day before.

A guy who looked like he could have been a biker, walked out of the store, past me and said, "Nice Bike."

I said, "Thanks."

He got into a red pickup truck and drove away.

Five minutes later, the red pickup truck pulled back into the parking lot, only now there were three guys in it, and nobody got out. They seemed to be watching me, but whenever I would look at them, they would look away.

I was getting a bad feeling about this. I had my Glock in the little saddle bag on the left side of the bike and contemplated whether to get it out.

Fifteen minutes later, I finished the water, and they were still sitting there.

Taking my time, I packed away my map, put my jacket back on and got the pistol out of my saddlebag and put it in my belt holster.

Firing up the chopper, I pulled out onto Main Street, watching my rear-view mirrors to see if the red pickup followed, but thankfully they did not.

Turning right on 1st Street, I followed it north till it led out of town on Hwy 64, all the while keeping a lookout for that truck. Hwy 64 was now a four-lane divided road, and even after getting well clear of town, I kept my head on a swivel.

I enjoy going through small towns, getting the feel of middle America, real people living real lives. But some people can be a bit too real, and I was happy that Clayton was not a town where I had planned to spend the night.

There were now long straight stretches of grasslands with cattle decorating the landscape like large black beetles. As the road turned northwest, the elevation rose to over six thousand feet. The temperature became cooler and with the wind more to my back, the riding was a pleasure.

Another gas stop was in the little, old, and almost deserted village of Des Moines, New Mexico.

Estimated population of one-hundred and twenty-two as of 2019.

Hwy 64 was now a four-lane undivided highway, and just outside of town is the Goodnight-Loving Trail rest area. The famous cattle drive trail crosses Hwy 64 at this location.

The trail is named after legendary Texas ranchers Charles Goodnight and Oliver Loving. They were the models for Woodrow Call and Gus McCrae in Larry McMurtry's bestselling and Pulitzer Prize winning novel, Lonesome Dove. The mini-series is one of the best westerns ever made.

Charles Goodnight, while a Texas Ranger, rescued Cynthia Ann Parker (Mother of Quanah) from the Comanches in 1860, which I mentioned earlier in this book.

It was getting late, and the temperatures were cooling down as I rode into Raton, New Mexico. I am very familiar with the town since I had been shooting rifle competitions at the huge NRA Whittington Center just outside of town for the last eighteen years.

The Robin Hood motel was a place I had stayed before, and I was happy to find they had a room, and while checking, in I met another motorcycle rider.

Seeing his bike in the parking lot from a distance I asked, "Is that a BMW?"
He said, "No, it's a Triumph Trophy, their touring bike."

I said, "Looks nice, all that wind protection must make it easy to go long distances. Where are you coming from?"

"North Carolina."

"Man, you're a long way from home."

"Yeah, but home is Seattle, Washington, I'm on my way back. Where is a good place to eat here?"

"Other than fast food, probably K-Bobs, just down the street. That's where I'm going, why don't you join me, and we can talk about our travels."

He did, and we did. His name was Thatch, and his ten-thousand-mile ride made my little three-thousand-miles look like a walk in the park. He was on his third rear tire for this trip alone.

It was a pleasant conversation with a likeminded person. He asked if I had gotten much rain, I said none, I had been lucky so far. He said he had been rained on a lot. My luck was about to change.

After dinner I jumped back on the bike and made a trip to the Whittington Center about ten miles out of town to see my friend and fellow author H.L. Anderson, he works the night shift there.

We had an enjoyable visit, having not seen each other for a while due to the covid situation.

The Whittington Center is a wonderful place to visit, they have cabins, RV and tent camping. Plus all sorts of wildlife like deer, antelope, black bear, wild turkey and elk can often be see alongside the road.

Soon it was back to the Robin Hood motel for some much-needed sleep.

The world's best shooting range

Day 15

New Mexico

There were plenty of places to eat breakfast, like the Oasis Diner, but when I finally got the bike repacked, I was anxious to be on my way and rode out of town.

Again, on Hwy 64, I stopped by the Whittington Center one more time to visit with some other friends, this time from the Fifty Caliber Shooters Association. President Randy Powell and world class shooter John Buhay were there to shoot an ELR, Extreme Long-Range competition, hitting targets as far as two miles away.

Raton is right on Interstate 25. I could have taken the usual fast route, south to I-40 and then west to I-17, but I was not ready to give in to the super slab just yet.

I was still in a back road frame of mind.

Heading west on Hwy 64, I knew there was a cafe in the small town of Cimarron, but when I went by, the sign said it was closed, so I pressed on, happy to be heading into higher, cooler country.

Randy, the author, and John at the Whittington Center in the wilds of New Mexico.

Mountains were ahead, and with that, pine trees and twisty roads with a river alongside. I had been riding through the plains and farmland for so long, it was a treat get into some nice country for a change.

Winding my way up Hwy 64, I would find myself on this same road the entire day. Or at least I should have been.

It was three-hundred miles to my destination of Farmington, NM for the night. Most all of it riding through mountains.

As all of you motorcycle riders out there know, one of the sometimes-wonderful things about being on a bike are the smells. Passing a steakhouse or a Burger King. Newly mowed grass or alfalfa. Riding alongside the ocean or in this case, crisp mountain air and pine trees.

Then, there are times when it is not so wonderful. Like following diesel trucks, or passing cattle stockyards, large chicken ranches, a sewer plant, or roadkill, like a dead skunk.

Like life, you have to take the bad with the good. But you are out in the world, experiencing (if not enjoying) it all.

It was not long before I stopped to take pictures. In Cimarron Canyon State Park, I pulled off at the spectacular Palisades Sill, alongside the Cimarron River. Elevation, eight thousand feet.

It is a beautiful spot with pine trees and cottonwoods and towering solid rock cliffs just on the other side of the river. Jutting straight up about five-hundred feet above the road.

Trout fisherman wearing waders were standing in the river, casting their lines right beside the highway, which was not busy, just one car or truck every few minutes.

It was not very secluded, but it still felt that way, being one of the most peaceful spots I had seen on my trip so far.

The Palisades Sill

I almost wished I had time to pitch my tent and stay a while.

As the elevation got higher, the countryside got more scenic, and the twisty roads turned tighter and more fun. But I kept the speed down because this bike was a low rider.

Once you run out of lean angle, if you are going too fast, you are not going to make a curve, no matter how good a rider you are.

When hard parts start dragging and digging into the pavement, it lifts the tires off the road and suddenly you have no traction. You are either forced to go wide, or the bike falls out from under you, and you are sliding out of control.

Doing that on a curve, is never a good idea!

I had seen this happen twice in the seventies, two friends and brothers on low riders and trying to keep up with faster bikes could not make curves.

One, on an inside curve, went wide and hit a Jeep head-on.

I took this picture after the rider went wide and hit the Jeep head-on

The other was on an outside curve. He went off a cliff. Both riders were right behind me when these incidents happened.

Amazingly, neither were wearing helmets, but both survived. We normally never wore helmets back then, except in states where they were required.

Today, helmets make a lot of sense to me. They provide protection from the sun and reduce wind noise in my ears. Plus, every time I've had a large bug or a rock smack into the helmet or face shield, I smile, happy to have the protection.

And then there is the rain...

Someone once told me, "You must learn from the mistakes of others. You will never live long enough to make them all yourself."

I like to corner hard and lean over on the twisty mountain roads, but I don't try to do it on a motorcycle that is not made for it.

The sound of foot-pegs or floorboards scraping are usually your first warning of leaning too far. If they start dragging, they are like curb-finders (remember those?), warning you are close to your maximum lean angle.

Keeping that in mind, I kept the pace nice and slow. Straying into the path of an oncoming car or rocketing off a cliff into mid-air would have put a crimp in my travel plans.
Getting to my destination for the day was my goal and I did not want to ruin it by being in a hurry.

As I went higher, it got cooler, and the roads got twistier. It was great riding! An hour and a half after leaving Raton, I was descending on a curving road behind a long line of cars with a motorhome in the lead.

A wide valley was ahead with the blue expanse of Eagle Nest Lake dominating the scenic view.

Once in the town of Eagle Nest, I stopped at three cafes or saloons before I found one that was open. It was across from the city park.

It felt odd walking down the wood sidewalk and into the old saloon. My cowboy boots thumped on the wooden floors, I felt like I should also be wearing a Stetson hat and carrying a six-gun.

 A large bar took up one side of the room, and to make matters worse, I was ordering coffee instead of beer or whiskey.

Oh well, it was past noon, and I still had a long way to ride today.
After ordering a grilled chicken sandwich, it was nice to relax in the saloon, with its dark wooden floors, walls, and ornate bar, enjoying the old west setting in this beautiful, quaint mountain town.

Before leaving town, I pulled into a Shell station to fill up. Soon I was following Hwy 64 around the lake, out of town southbound heading for Taos.

Eagle Nest, New Mexico

Once again, I was climbing out of a valley into another mountain range with curves, switchbacks, and blind corners.

As I have said before, in the mountains and forests I always worry about deer and elk and their warped sense of humor.

It was a beautiful ride, and I was enjoying the journey.

The distance was only thirty-two miles from Eagle Nest to Taos, but it took me almost an hour. Frequent hairpin turns marked twenty miles per hour made me keep the pace down.

Descending into the valley, it got warmer, and by the time I got into Taos, it was hot.

Because it is a very old town, the streets are narrow, and it does not take much traffic to create slow going.

I had been there many times and had no desire to stop and look around. Finally getting to the traffic light downtown, Hwy 64 took a right and so did I.
The Ultima motor was stuttering and complaining at the slow pace, echoing between the buildings.

I worked my way through the old streets, occasionally looking into store windows and seeing an apparition of a lone rider in the reflection of the glass.

Having just gassed up at Eagle Nest, I did a very unusual thing... I passed open gas stations.

That was my first mistake of the day.

I also passed the sign for the turn to the Taos Pueblo. A dwelling that had been in constant habitation for over one thousand years.
I had been there before.

Eventually, the traffic got lighter and there were crops, pastures, and lush cottonwood trees lining the highway. I was warily eyeing the dark clouds to the west, knowing as the day wore on, they would get darker, and I would get wet.

Not far out of town, there was a four-way traffic light. It looked like straight ahead would take me west, the way I wanted to go. So straight I went.

My Shovel-Head chopper at the Taos Pueblo in 1973

Half an hour and twenty-two miles later as the road climbed into the mountains, those dark clouds started to rain.

Finally reaching a town, I pulled into the first gas station I saw. Hoping to get out of the rain I parked next to the pumps under the awning, but the rain was coming in sideways.

After filling up and hopping back on the bike, I was in a hurry because of the heavy slanting raindrops, but my foot caught on the pack that I lean on.

The momentum of me standing the bike up brought it upright, but I was unable to put my foot down on the right side.

I started falling to the right, with my right foot caught under me. Instantly I had visions of crashing down onto the concrete, in the pouring rain and not being able to pick up the bike or getting trapped underneath it.

Going into full panic mode, just as we were falling to the right, somehow, I was able to free my right foot and get it down just in time.

Sweating and panting, I looked around to see if anyone had seen that near crisis, but no one was paying any attention. They did not look past the heavy rain on their windshields. If I had fallen, I was ready to do a Pee Wee Herman and say, "I did that on purpose."

I started the bike and pulled it into the leeward side of the convenience store. It was relatively dry there, so I parked the bike and got out my map, then went inside.

Seeing an older lady behind the counter, I asked, "Where am I?"

With a twinkle in her eye, she said, "Standing in my store."

"Okay, well, what town is your store in?"

She laughed, "This is Questa, and you are in the Sangre De Cristo Mountains."

Thanking her, I checked my map, kicking myself for thinking I had made a second mistake of the day.

I should have made a left at that light. That was Hwy 64. I accidentally got on Hwy 522, and the elevation here in Questa was seven thousand, five hundred feet.

If I kept going straight, I would climb higher and higher until I was in Colorado. It probably would have been snowing by then.

Still with a long way to go for the day, I got back on the bike and headed southbound again. The rain I had ridden through on the way up, was still there on the way down. I got soaked for an hour for nothing.

On the way up I passed a guy hitchhiking north, the way I was going. I waved to him.

One the way back I passed him again, this time he was hitchhiking southbound. I waved to him again.

Finally arriving at the intersection and the lower elevation, the rain had stopped for now and I was grateful to turn right, back onto Hwy 64, now westbound.

Before long I was crossing the Rio Grande Gorge Bridge, at six-hundred and fifty feet above the Rio Grande River. It is the fifth highest bridge in the United States Highway System.

Riding over the very scenic vistas, there were a lot of tourists on the bridge taking pictures of the deep canyon with the river below.

Being behind schedule I kept moving, I already have pictures from having been there in 1973.

In the lower altitude and warmer air, I was starting to dry out. Just past the gorge, Hwy 64 turned north, and the chopper and I charged past The Greater World Earthship Community on the right side of the road.

With more time, I would have loved to tour the place. It is a random collection of the most unique, efficient, and environmentally friendly homes I have ever seen.

The people who build them are as much artists as they are architects. You can see many of these homes from the road, which is all I did as I tried to make up lost time.

After that, on the long straight stretch of 64, I was further entertained by getting rained on again. I had almost dried out, but it was not to be.

Seeing signs that said Tres Piedras, I was sure they would have gas. After all, they had their own sign!

There had been no stations since I left Questa.

Coming to the intersection of Tres Piedras, where 64 crosses Hwy 285, I stopped at the stop sign and looked in vain for a station only to see none.

There was a building that looked like it used to be one but was no longer, it had been abandoned. Out of business for whatever reason.

My heart sank as I accelerated up the road into the Carson National Forest, hoping that I would find a gas station somewhere up in those cloudy, dark, brooding mountains ahead of me.

I had already gone forty-seven miles, about half the range of my tank, and had not seen a single station.

I started having unpleasant visions of running out of gas on the top of a mountain and being soaking wet in a freezing rainstorm.

Forty-seven miles to a car or truck is nothing when you can hold twenty gallons of gas. For motorcycles that hold five or six gallons, you are still good. When you have three, it is a different story.

I pressed on into the mountains.

As I went higher, it got darker and colder. The country was beautiful, but I was no longer interested in enjoying it. I was to find there was not a single town or community for the next fifty miles.

To add to the fun, the rain was back and now the temperature was dropping and the altitude over the summit was just under eight thousand feet.

When the cold got to be too much, I stopped in an empty picnic area and started unpacking my gear to get a sweatshirt and my rain jacket.

No cars or trucks went by, which made me wonder, if I ran out of gas, how much help would there be? I was freezing cold, and my hands were numb and shook as I pulled on my rain jacket and struggled to put my pack back together.

All would not be lost if I had to spend the night on that mountain, I was not totally unprepared; I had a tent, sleeping bag and air mattress. But you might think I would have brought an emergency gas can too.

With numb shaking fingers, I checked my phone to see where the next gas was, but there was no reception.

The paper map said the next town was Tierra Amarilla, big enough to be on a map, but there was no way to know if they had gas.

I prayed a little as I turned the key, and my trusty chopper fired up on cue, just like always.

I was beginning to love this bike.

The view tube gas gauge on the side of my tank showed about an inch worth of gas. Fortunately, after my stop, I was on the western slope of the mountain range and the ride was all downhill.

Mostly at idle, trying to stretch the gas, I nursed the bike out of the mountains. But as I got to lower elevations, the roads flattened out and I needed to use more power.

Soon the visible gas in the tube disappeared and I waited for the engine to sputter so I could go onto the reserve setting. I had no Idea how far that would take me.

Coming to a stop sign, I turned right where Hwy 64 merged with Hwy 84 and headed north. After about four miles, I was delighted to see a gas station, and yes, it was even open. I could not believe I had made it.

My odometer said ninety-seven point five miles from Questa, the last place I had gassed up after my wrong turn.
I had just ridden through some of the most beautiful country of my whole trip and had not been able to appreciate any of it because I was

too stressed out about the gas, and the rain, and the cold.

Ironically, not having gotten gas in Taos, I would have surely run out if I had not made that wrong turn and ended up in Questa. From Eagle Nest to Tierra Amarilla was one-hundred, thirty-five miles and there is no way I would have made it.

Inside, I bought a bottle of water and thanked the young lady behind the counter for having a gas station here.

She looked at me like I was from California, and hesitantly said, "No Problem."

It was warm again and had stopped raining. I finished the water and got my rain jacket packed back onto the bike. I could feel my fingers again. Studying my paper map, it looked like Chama was only fifteen miles up the road.

It was five thirty in the afternoon, so the question was, do I stay in Chama? Or press on to my planned destination of Farmington, another one-hundred and twenty-four miles.

Google Maps said it would take two hours and twenty minutes, but for me, with one more gas stop, I knew it would be closer to three hours. I pressed on.

Just before Chama, 64 turned left to the west and I went with it. With the sun getting low in the afternoon sky, I passed through more small forgotten towns that were now so familiar in New Mexico.

It is sad, but at the same time, you must admire the people that stay and stick it out. What would they rather do, move to Chicago or Los Angeles?

Hell no! I am sure they are right where they want to be. Where many have grown up, where their families and friends are.

After the turn it was only twenty-seven miles to the small town of Dulce. Seeing a gas station, I bolted into it, whether I needed it or not. It turned out to be completely automated with nobody around.

The gas pumps, at least mine, pumped slowly, about a half a gallon per minute. I only needed about a gallon.

Dulce is home to the Jicarilla Apache Nation, and they had a nice casino with hotels rooms advertised on a big marque right on Hwy 64.

It was already seven o'clock, and the sun was still up. The summer solstice, the longest day of the year, had been just a couple of days prior. That sun was going to be up for a while, and I was going to be riding into it.

I contemplated stopping for the day. That would have been the smart thing to do, although I was not ready to give up yet. And besides, it was not raining. There were clouds to the west, but I had already been wet today, and was willing to take my chances.

I rolled the bike away from the pumps, and rearranged my gear on a picnic table, then I turned the camera on myself for the only time on this trip and made a short GoPro video, telling where I was and where I was going.

With the day's combination of heat, wet and cold, and the stress of finding gas stations, fatigue was starting to follow me as surely as my shadow as I rode into the afternoon sun.

I would rather ride with the sun in my eyes than to have it at my back, and have cars and trucks coming at me with the sun in their eyes. I trust my own capabilities more.

After Dulce, Hwy 64 turned south and then west again, once again I had the road mostly to myself.

It was beautiful country with more impressive emptiness. The open terrain was mostly sage brush and juniper trees.

I could not help but wonder if the only people who think we are over-populating the planet live in cities.

As I headed west, in the distance, a little to the left were storm clouds. Bright white on the top, bubbling up into the blue afternoon sky, and brooding dark underneath, with occasional flashes of lightning.

To the right of that was the late afternoon sun, slanting lower and lower. As long as I was heading southwest, it was not directly in front of me. If I was in the shadow of a mountain, which there were many, I got some relief.

Just before the community of Blanco, on the San Juan River, Hwy 64 followed some impressive rock formations. Weaving through shallow canyons of granite like a Mini Grand Canyon. It was a beautiful ride but didn't last long.

Blanco was a quiet little community, like so many places where it is easy to imagine yourself living there. But they didn't have gas, and I didn't stop.

Although I had planned to be in Farmington that night, this was the first day I fell short of my goal.

By eight thirty I entered the town of Bloomfield with the sun just setting and annoyingly shining in my eyes. I decided I'd had enough for the day.

Bloomfield is the biggest town I had seen since Chama. I could also see fast food and restaurants; I decided this place would do and started looking for a cheap motel.

Cruising through town, squinting into the sun, I checked out the places to stay, and to eat.

Passing the little Bloomfield Motel, it looked like it would do. I made a U-turn and went back. As I preferred, they had rooms where you could park right in front of your door. The price was right, and I was in for the night.

By the time I unloaded the bike, the young lady behind the desk said the restaurants would all be closed. It was nine o'clock and only fast food remained, and it just happened there was a Burger King across the main highway.

I risked my life crossing that four-lane highway, twice. Actually, it was not that bad. It was late and traffic was light, and I found I cannot run like I used to. Especially after sitting on my ass on a vibrating motorcycle all day.

The Double Whopper with Cheese was great, and there was a liquor store next door that had vodka and orange juice. After the life I have led, sleep doesn't come easy at night, even after a long hard day, but now I was totally set for the night.

Since starting out this morning, I had crossed almost all the northern part of the state of New Mexico, most of it in mountainous terrain, and all of it with either heat, wet, or cold.
It was great to relax and get horizontal for the first time in about sixteen hours.

Day 16

The Hyperspace Interstate

After enjoying several cups of free coffee and a muffin in the lobby of the motel, I packed the bike and figured I would find a little cafe or diner along my route of travel.

I rode the bike around the corner to a gas station and filled up, then I was back on 64, heading west again, apprehensively watching the overcast skies with some storm clouds on the horizon.

Fifteen minutes later I was picking my way through the traffic in Farmington, New Mexico. It was morning rush hour, which was pleasantly not a big deal compared to any big city.

No cafes caught my attention, so I kept going.

Thirty miles later I was in the town of Shiprock, where I stopped to top off. I didn't need gas, but the question of when it would be available again made me want to keep the tank full.

After the third day of riding west on Hwy 64, I finally turned southbound on Hwy 491 which opened up into a four-lane divided highway.

491 was mostly smooth and pleasant, and the traffic moved right along. It was not an interstate, but you might have thought it was. This was no country road.

About ten miles south of the town of Shiprock, I stopped alongside the road to take a picture of the huge rock monument from which the town got its name.

Pioneers had named the rock formation "Shiprock" because it looked like a ship plowing through the ocean, bow wave and all. It is just as convincing when seen from the air.

The weather was not looking any better, so at a gas stop I put on my rain jacket. Back on the road, blasting down Hwy 491, I was once again riding against the wind, getting buffeted by a headwind out of the south.

On a motorcycle, the wind is inevitably your friend, or your nemesis. Usually the latter.

Shiprock from the air

Shiprock from Hwy 491

With my cheap, loose fitting rain jacket flapping in the wind, I watched the storm clouds come closer with their long curtains of rain reaching to the ground.

Riding into one of those curtains, the downpour started. Visibility became difficult as the water built up on my face shield, while cars and trucks kicked up a spray of water in front of me that was more like a fog, often limiting visibility to a few yards.

It was not long before my pants were soaked, and my gloves and boots were wet. But the rain jacket kept my torso and arms dry and warm.

After about five miles I came out the other side of the storm and before long I was drying out. Until I hit another wall of water to repeat the process.

After four soakings and drying out, I came into the north side of Gallup, New Mexico. Civilization again.

Not stopping for gas or food, I took on the traffic until reaching Interstate 40, where I turned west and pressed on.

For this whole trip I had been avoiding interstate highways, wanting to feel like the old days of riding a motorcycle around the country on mostly two-lane roads.

Even riding through Texas and Oklahoma, some of the bigger four-lane highways frequently go through the middle of towns instead of bypassing them.

I had planned to return to the scenic route of the first days of my trip along the Mogollon Rim, (pronounced Muggy-on), but summer fires had closed many of the roads in that area. Trying to go that way would not be wise.

Other than going further north on Hwy 160, through the Navajo Nation and the heat of the painted desert, I-40 seemed to be the only way.

Okay Interstate... Here I come.

On the super slab, I was speeding along in my own personal time warp. Riding hour after hour, left to my own imagination, I started fantasizing about rocketing through space.

Your surroundings come at you and then fall away like stars in hyperspace as you bypass dying planets where life still goes on but is ignored by the speeding travelers passing nearby.

On those little planets are where the life is happening. Missing that life, is like missing life itself. Soon, will we be using Star Trek's Transporters? Where we would miss the traveling experience all together?

I kept myself entertained by dodging around the lumbering sub-space semi-trucks. They were not traveling at the speed of light like I was.

I was charging into the buffeting wind, and feeling the vibration of a radical chopper, revving three thousand plus RPM's at eighty-five miles per hour. The bike was belching a roaring contrail of noise behind it.

As I bounced down the rough highway it felt very little like zooming through hyperspace.

But I tried to enjoy the fantasy, occupying my mind as I sped down the interstate that I didn't want to be on.

The bike never failed me. I depended on her, and she came through every time. Started every time. Ran all day long, every day. Through heat and rain and sometimes heavy traffic.

She proved to me that I could depend on her. As she depended on me.

It is hard not to think of machines like this as real entities. I have always felt that way, and as the years pass that feeling seems to grow stronger.

I spent years riding horses, together you can do things you cannot do on your own; You trust your horse and your horse learns to trust you. A symbiotic partnership, you develop a bond.

Transferring that to motorcycles seems a natural progression to me. But then... Maybe I am crazy.

We have all heard that life is a journey.
'Enjoy the journey.'
'It's all about the journey, not the destination.'

So, if life is the journey, what is the destination?

The coffin? The funeral? The grave? Death?

If we associate a motorcycle ride with life, then the destination is like dying, and the ride is life itself.

Where do we want to put our focus on our life?

The ride? Or the destination?

I like to think it is me and the bike, being as one. I am part of her, she is part of me, journeying through life together. Depending on each other. Experiencing life. The destination can wait.

These are the kind of thoughts that occupied my mind as I droned down the long boring interstate.

The bike is happy at eighty miles per hour. The vibration smooths out and the six-speed transmission makes a big difference.

Leaning back against my gear, I am comfortable. It's like sitting in an easy chair in your living room with an eighty mile an hour fan blowing on you.

If you are traveling at eighty, and you have a twenty mile per hour headwind, it feels like you are going one hundred miles per hour. Turn around, and it feels like you are only doing sixty.

It is always nicer to be gone with the wind than against it.

It does not take long to get places on the interstate. Soon I was crossing the state line back into Arizona where the Chief Yellow Horse trading post is. I pulled into the Speedy's Truck Stop to top off the tank again.

Speedy's had a restaurant and I debated having lunch, but the call of the highway was too strong.

I did not want to spend the night just a few hours from home, today would be my longest one-day ride on this trip.

From Bloomfield, New Mexico to home would be just under four-hundred miles. A piece of cake on an Electra Glide, or a BMW, but on a chopper with my seventy-year-old body, I had to push hard to make it work.

On my way back to the interstate I stopped to take a couple of pictures of the Teepee Trading post. Mostly abandoned since the whole virus panic-demic. The enormous granite mountain behind it made for scenic photos, and the sadly deserted buildings made it look like something out of the distant past.

The once thriving Tee Pee Trading Post on I-40.

This was the third week in June 2021 and the Pacific Northwest had been having a major heatwave. One hundred and thirteen-degrees Fahrenheit for a high in Seattle, Washington and Portland, Oregon.

Out ahead of me was still most of the Navajo Nation, the Painted Desert, and Petrified Forest. I was concerned that the temperatures were going to be hot, but luck was with me, as usual, and those clouds that had been nice enough to rain on me earlier were still lurking about.

Instead of being over the hundred-degree mark, the temps were only in the mid-nineties, and it was tolerable especially as long as you are moving along with that eighty-five mile per hour fan on you.

Just down the road is the tiny town of Houck, Arizona which is famous for its re-creation of Fort Courage, from the "F-Troop" television show in the sixties.

What's left of America, for sale.

Set up for tourists and kids, it used to get a lot of attention. I had passed it a hundred times but never stopped. Finally, this time I did.

Like so many businesses after the pandemic, it is now just a shell, another relic of the past. Gone are the clicking of camera shutters and the excited laughter of children finally getting out of the car on long road trips, eating ice cream and marveling at the facade of the old west.

Fort Courage, Houck, Arizona

Fort Courage was an odd mix of isolation and noise, with the busy Interstate 40 just on the other side of the frontage road which itself is a section of old Route 66.

Next stop, Holbrook, Arizona. Getting gas, I wrote down the miles and gallons used like I had been doing every day on this journey. I also frequently made notes on some of my thoughts while riding so I would not forget.

I stopped at the first gas station, away from the crowds at the fast-food joints over on the west side of town. Holbrook sits in the middle of the Petrified Forest National Park. I was distracted by the vast expanses of land extending to the horizon in all directions. It is difficult to describe the emptiness.

I had to step back and take a picture.

The middle of nowhere, which is actually Holbrook, Arizona.

Soon back into hyperspace as I blasted down the interstate, I felt a tug on my jacket pocket where I kept my little notebook.

Touching it with my gloved hand, it felt like the notebook was still there, I had forgotten to close the pocket, so I zipped it up and pressed on.

From Holbrook to Flagstaff was ninety miles, with long stretches of no gas stations, so it made sense to stop in Winslow to top off.

There I found I had lost my little notebook, with all the information about my trip. It might have made sense to go back right then, and try to find it, but I felt that odd mix of wanting to get home, and not wanting the trip to end.

Plus, there was the fatigue. Hours of battling the winds and rough roads can wear you down.

I got back on the interstate and continued westbound.

There were storm clouds again and I got rained on a couple more times in Arizona, but they were brief, and I dried out quickly.

Traffic in Flagstaff was busy, so I was on my toes knowing that every driver was out to get me. But I foiled them and made it through anyway.

Turning south on Interstate 17, the ride from Flagstaff is all downhill. Traffic runs fast and the roads are always rough because of the freezing temperatures during the winter. At least today, at this high altitude it was pleasant, not hot, not cold.

The curves coming down the mountain were fast and fun, and as usual the bike ran great.

I got to the Verde Valley, which in summertime is typically over one hundred degrees, even though it is one-hundred miles north of Phoenix, it felt the same as the heat in that big city.

Home

As I approached home, I started to become uneasy, wishing I had some new place to go instead of being happy the journey was ending, I felt a bit sad.

The sun was setting as I pulled into my long driveway and into my garage.

It was good to be back, and not to have to spend all day vibrating down the road with the wind battering you back and forth. Trying to decide where to eat, if you ate at all, or just keep heading down the road while you still have daylight.

For now, no more worrying about where the next gas station might be or if the bike would keep running. She performed flawlessly the whole trip. I was proud of her, like a father of a kid.

She got me there and back. I got her there and back. We were a team.

She coughs and sputters and complains at low speeds, she steers hard with that front end, and twenty-one-inch wheel, she leaks oil and rides as smooth as an old buckboard wagon, but I wouldn't trade her for the newest, most modern interstate cruise missile for anything.

End of the road. For now.

I'm already looking over my wrinkled, torn and well-worn paper maps, trying to figure out the next trip.

Acknowledgments

I would like to thank all of you readers, for buying this book, and coming along on this little trip with me. It is truly rewarding whenever people want to read what a writer has to say.

How can anyone ever really ride alone when so many likeminded people want to accompany you?

This book is about a simple ride, relatively free of drama. Only one accident which was not mine. No police chases, breakdowns, or conflicts.

I would also like to thank, "Indian Dave" for building a great motorcycle in 2007. He is the one who worked out most of the kinks. Then my friend and Brother Hangmen James, who sold it to me.
"Sorry Bro, you can't have her back just yet."

Thank you to my proofreaders for helping me with the first draft of this manuscript.
And thank you to Amazon, and their Kindle Direct Publishing, giving me a platform to publish my books.

Update on Juan and Bubba

After hitting the pothole and crashing in Eufaula, Oklahoma, Juan spent a week in the hospital getting surgery on both arms. Back in Arizona, he was recovering well, but Juan is an impatient young man, as soon as the cast was off, it was not completely healed and he promptly broke his left arm again.

Shattering the humerus and popping out all the screws they had installed the first time.

Going in for emergency repairs a second time, he got fixed up again. Fortunately, his body is still under warranty.

As of this writing, he is promising to be good, and not push it. He should be back riding another motorcycle as soon as we allow him to.

Bubba, who only received cuts and bruises, is fine and back on the road on a new bike.

About the Author

Born in Florida, the youngest of four children, the family moved to California when he was seven. After that family broke up, as a teenager the author struck out on his own.

Dropping out of high school, he continued his education at the school of hard knocks, falling into life in an outlaw motorcycle club which he wrote about in his first book, 'Hangmen.'

He eventually worked his way into aviation jobs, becoming a Captain, flying for American Airlines.

In later life, he became a competition rifle shooter, earning multiple world championships and world records while shooting the big .50 BMG rifles.

He has also lived in Alaska, Texas and Arizona where he resides now.

Today, his passion is writing.

Printed in Great Britain
by Amazon